Wa

G000124722

Back

Then...

Street Poetry in Motion

Mr Banton
Wayne Bayley

British Library Cataloguing in Publication Data: A catalogue record for this book is available from the British Library.

ISBN: 9798799709365.

Book cover design: Pixaby.

Editor: Joy Smart.

Proofreader: Joy Smart.

Disclaimer:

This book is written in street
slang vernacular.

Table of Contents

Dedication

This book is dedicated to my grandpa
Jim Bayley, the Universe R.I.P.

Introduction

As most of you will know, my name is Wayne Bayley also known as Mr. Banton and I am a Poet.

I wrote these rhymes a very long time ago and I've never had apart from once or twice at an open mic performance the opportunity share them, I just sat back and said nothing and kept them inside for a long while.

Since 2nd May 2004, I have wanted to write a book, so

better late than never. I finally decided to put them in a book because I wanted my poems to be heard. I just wanted to explain and express myself how I was feeling way back then and see my rhymes on paper. Welcome to Wayne's world. Always go after your dreams.

Mr. Banton aka Wayne Bayley

Acknowledgements

First and foremost, thank you to the Most High God that has sustained me and kept me thus far.

Secondly, I would like to take this time to thank everyone who donated to my Go Fund Me book campaign. I am able to realise my long-lost dream of becoming an author and sharing my heartfelt poetical expression with the world, because you sowed a seed.

Your generous donations have enabled me to start a new

book business which has the potential to go global and for that I will forever be grateful.

I would love to thank my family on both sides, my mum and dad for believing in my first book. I would also like to thank my aunties, uncles and people who supported me in publishing my debut books. Special thanks to my grandad Jim Bayley 'The Boss' Rest in Peace. Thanks to my cousin Winnie for helping me put this book together and making my dream a reality.

Material Things
Reflections

Material Things was the first poem I ever wrote, and it was at my cousin Winnie's house on the 2nd of May 2004.

Growing up as a youth from Leyton, East London, there were a lot of things that I glorified. Money was the first, females were the second, fast cars and jewellery were the third and raving and going out to house parties came in last.

When I sat down and really analysed my environment and what was going on around me, the things I was seeing on the television and the music I was hearing on the radio, I came up with this poem material things.

Years down the line, my cousin Winnie was doing all these great, wonderful things in the publishing world, seeing her writing and making people's ideas become real to the page was dope and that was something really positive to witness her see the BIG TIME. I love you fam, keep on doing your ting cuz, making your younger cousins proud.

Peace, love and respect.

Wayne

Material Things

Material Things, possessions you can't take when you die.

Thinking why life's so f**ked up?

Open your eyes my brother, are you so blind?

Can you not see the project before thee?

Yo, it's one big trap, so hard to react.

So don't relax buying Prada, Gucci and Fendi tux.

I tried to explain, you still remain in that same old same, material game.

Can't you hear what's happening, let alone, see?

Material infecting my black community.

His drop top Benz and his six carat ring.

Surely gonna help him f**k that buff ting.

Glamour and glory that's what you adore.

Can that come with you when death is at your door.

Surely not man, so let's be wise.

Don't let material fool your eyes.

Eyes send messages straight to the brain.

Don't let material drive you insane.

Keep your mind strong, don't let it suffer.

Always be willing to help our Black brother.

The Wind
Reflections

This poem The Wind, came to me when I was out on a freezing cold winter's day. It was hard for me to walk against the windy breeze and around that time my girlfriend I was with was in America chasing her music career, however we used to talk on the phone every other day or so. I told her this poem and she liked it.

Months down the line, we kind of lost contact and a new girl came into my life and her name was Windin. Her nickname that was, and she was a special girl. I leave it for you to work out. I met her on the seventh month of the year.

Her birthday was on the 27th of the first of the month 1977.

Her phone number had a bag of sevens, in it.

What more can I say, for all those who didn't hit the nail on the head.

She was my direct link from God. A good-hearted genuine person, and I wrote this poem long before I met her. So when I thought about it, the poem, the girl, it kind of worked out. So here it is.

The Wind

The wind flows I imagine it be me.

Flowing from town to town on top of the blue sea.

How safe and sound I imagined the wind to be.

Flowing through the leaves of the brown log tree.

From country to country at the speed of light.

You can't see me, you can feel me more times at night.

If the season ain't right Jack Frost may bite.

Not the type of season to be flying a kite.

You see, some people love me, others show hate.

I'll show them that I'm great.

When the heat starts to break.

100 degrees my mate humid comes along.

They hate me when I'm here and beg me when I'm gone.

My friend called the sun the most powerful source.

When it's blooming, have you fuming and assuming where the wind at?

Then I breeze through, kindly greet you.

Gently treat you, cool down my people.

We're all equal on mother's earth.

Every day there's death and every day there's birth.

So you've got to think first of repeated action.

A fraction of the brain can bring a lot of gain.

And my name's Wayne.

Thug Cry
Reflections

Thug Cry was written because there was a lot of things I started to understand about the world and how it's run. There was a revelation about myself and family members from both sides.

One of my brethren Chubby Dred gets shot outside his house in Leytonstone and nearly loses his life.

That was a madness, some real f**ked up s**t.

My next brethren Twiggy gets bored and dies in Leyton, which was some real shocking news when I heard it, cos Twiggy was my dawg. I did not know what to think.

He had a big funeral and Movado made a tune for him. So R.I.P, bad man Twiggy.

Still, amongst all of that, my next brethren got shot outside of rave in East London, and nearly dies. However, with the Grace of God Mr. Mittoo made it through, how about that? Living to tell the tale.

I also lost my girl, who decided to move to the United States after an eight-year relationship.

She wanted me to move there with her, however I just wasn't ready to do what she had done and that was leave everything behind.

America is a country I know nothing about, nothing what so ever.

But if she had said the right words to me, the ones I wanted to hear, I would of had no choice.

But for some reason, it didn't go that way and way back then, I didn't understand anything.

I trusted no one.

I was on edge every single day and every second of my life. My pully too.

Everything in my head was all jumbled up, trying to make sense of it all. My life was real hard.

I've cried a couple of times and I ain't ashamed to say it.

Hear this…

Thug Cry

Have you ever seen a thug cry?

Deep down his heart's hurting.

Emotion and feelings f**ked up that's the first ting.

It could be anything.

This life of worry, struggle, stress brings less.

Most put on vests on their chest, avoid the burning flame.

It could be anything this life of pain.

Got to stay the same.

Could've just lost a loved one.

Know in your brain that you're never gonna to see them again.

Until you get there, wherever it be.

Spend your next years visiting a cemetery.

That's why it's necessary to watch your back whether legit or illegal.

This life s**t be lethal.

Check out my sequel.

What happen to them people?

Going on like they don't hear.

I just told them when a thug shed a tear.

Beware, start living in fear.

Cause I swear, some thugs don't care.

Start killing, so you better declare.

Father God hear this sinner's prayer.

Keep me clear of these bad mind devil dares or dare devils.

Want to see me six levels in the dirt.

But I disguise in a wig and skirt.

Fire splurt, some thugs put in work, man.

Anytime, anywhere drop and hurt man.

It's top rank pull a skank, point blank in ya.

When I see ya, take your money, ain't no thanking ya.

That's how it goes, road code, keep the links tight.

One slipping, all fall, got to think right.

Escape the flashing blue light into the dark night.

Disrespect anytime the matic sparks right.

That's how it goes.

We don't fear foes.

No, no.

Joy Reflections

This poem is called Joy, the reason I wrote it was because my mum is the light of my life and I love her so much. She always says she loves me more, because I came out of her and I'm a part of her flesh. She is older and wiser than me and I understand what she means. My love for her is still infinity as she is always a helpful mum and never forsaken me. Mum is the type of woman that will help you with whatever it is you want to do in life so long as it is not foolishness in her eyes. She is kind, very loving and a caring person who works her fingers to the bone all her life. As long as I can remember, my mum used to work in Walthamstow at the top of the market, Churchill, East 17. When my brother and I were just two and three years old.

My dad is a very different person. He was the provider for the family. Every Friday we would go shopping at the supermarket and get food, vegetables, and fruit for the house and that was our quality time together. All my dad cared about was his family obviously, but there were things which kept my dad level headed and that was cricket on Sunday's, 9-5 work, and going to the gym after work.

Mum always made sure dinner was ready on time and laid out on the table. Breakfast was always ready in the morning before school.

Homework was completed when we started secondary school. Clothes washed when dirty, we were kept clean. My precious Joy was always trying to keep our family tight in the best way she knew how. Her aim was to make you understand the situation on both sides. My mum was the only female in the house so she had a lot to contend with, thanks mum for all you continue to do, this one is for you. Hope you like it xxx.

Joy

Joy is great happiness.

Joy is great love.

If joy was a bird, she would be a white dove.

Joy is the meaning of conceiving your firstborn.

Control from birth.

Consider joy's worth.

Joy is the meaning of the youth of today.

You can pray for joy or have joy when you pray.

Each and every day, joy fights fears.

Just completed something you've been trying it in years.

Joy always cares.

Plus, she always shares.

Rich, poor, fat or slim.

Joy starts within.

Joy is a moral season and the reason for this song.

Once you seek Joy. compassion comes along.

But you got to stay strong.

When tears come near.

Be clear.

Ma dear, see joy be right
here.

When I see your face all I see
is grace.

On the chase to get her family
in place.

To return to the base of the
sun, where she first begun.

You done know I love my
mum.

Took her first breath on Jan
one.

And I'm her first son.

I'll show you how it's done, chum.

And my dad he'd be stamina.

Couldn't picture when he was slamming her.

A silent OG like a sperm meeting an ovary.

He told me, but never showed me.

I had to learn for myself, collecting all the wealth.

East 10 Reflections

The reason for this poem was because when I realised I was good at mixing and matching my words to make them rhyme, I wanted to represent for my hood. The place I grew up in was East 10 and East 11. If you asked me they are two different areas, but the same thing if you see what I mean. You see, one end of the road could be Leyton and the other Leytonstone. One road divided two areas and when everyone got older and everyone's P's (money) started to get bigger, attitude comes with how much P's you had. This man saying, I don't want to par with him because of this, another one saying he done that, so I don't want to be around him. You got other people chatting a lot of s**t, that is when I realized that it is only my family I could depend on in my time of need, and I wrote this about the hood I grew up in.

East 10

I'm from L.E.Y.T.O.N.E.T.E.N.

Beg no friend.

Certain friends always turn to foes.

You never know who's next to go, so…

Yo, mind how you roll.

These days life's a gamble.

We still scramble around town clocking Queen crown.

Every colour could be no other.

A long time discover as I
dwell on my brothers.

These are the colours I hustle
to get to.

Pink, purple, brown and blue.

You can't stop it, try stop it.

Never lock it.

Yo, one reach your socket.

You can't break my pocket.

My attitude is f**K it.

My brother, Bru split you in
two.

With one shot you get buckshot.

Make your blood clot.

Hope your blood rot.

We don't stop.

Fast like a roller coaster.

I'll ghost ya.

Rate, big boasters.

F**king well toast ya.

Straight like I'm burning bread.

Burn your head.

What with this burning lead.

You should have learnt
instead before you run up and
dead.

I'm a real G, yo, you gotta
feel me soul.

Rough Conspiracies Reflections

Around this time that I wrote Conspiracies I was going to a lot of open mics in Brixton, Southeast London. Back then it was all about the new revolution of being Black and positive. I was growing up as a youth at these shows. My dad and uncles used to have a sound system, so there was a lot of music playing on weekends. I mean, all types, Reggae, Calypso, Rare Groove, Soul, Revival, Hip

Hop, you name it, there was a collection. In my life, there was a time I realized about Rastafari and I started to love Rasta. This culture has always been in my life since a youngster because my uncle was a natty dread and the film Babylon was one I worshipped because as a youth, it puts your thoughts in a positive mind set and the Rasta culture has always been close to my heart and the HIGH GRADE weed too.

I started to hail the King from Ethiopia, the King of Kings and Lord of Lords, Jah Rastafari, Emmanuel *I,* Selassie I, that was me all day.

I started meditating about Black people and what we have gone through for centuries. It really made me reflect long and hard on our story. This is why I wrote this and told it to my brethren Chubby, who made a breakthrough in the music industry. When he heard it, he told me to be careful with what I'm saying, because it is a dangerous world out there. I went home and really checked what I was saying, but I didn't care, I just wanted to be heard. I attended an open mic at the Fridge Bar in Brixton and said the poem and got a good response. However, the only thing I did wrong after the poem was apologize. When I walked off stage a white woman approached me and told me, never apologize for anything you say on stage.

Then after that Kanye West brought out a tune called 'Can't Tell Me Nothing' and I listened to that on repeat. That is when I just decided I didn't want to do music anymore, I just wanted to forget I could even rhyme, and forget about music completely. That's what I did. (So this is the Hollah RN!)

Rough Conspiracies

When times get rough, can
you hold the stress?

When good turns bad do you
get depressed?

The rat race be fast so watch
how you step.

You might get tangled in life's
daily web.

Yo, lend me your ear, hear
this loud and clear.

There is a big conspiracy on
earth I swear.

Your wide asleep, try see beyond tomorrow.

The future enterprise leaves life in sorrow.

Run from the future and this global plan.

But where can you run, when you're in the devil's land?

Born in the belly but who lives in sin?

Blind up the people like Jesus' crucifixion.

When will you stop lying and tell the world the truth?

Allow free speech, stop misleading the youth.

The truth is there to be found.

Seek and you shall find.

A free-thinking mind is never on the grind.

Out here in the jungle what they call the city.

Got people live s**ty and you don't even pity.

You got the Prince's Trust now but I ain't trusting him.

His people robbed my people so I ain't never giving in.

Put the chain on the brain, so it's mental slavery.

Black people come together, we got to move bravely.

In this modern time designed to destroy your mind.

Hollow lead matic nine leave you way back in time.

Edited dictation be the wrong information.

What they give to live by, I don't live.

I'm just living, spell live backwards what do you get?

Life's a threat when you're
walking blindly.

Nothing in this world ain't
coming kindly.

Got to know the road you
choose, stay focused.

Some say it's really hopeless.

Dealing with the pressure that
arrives daily.

Can't move strayly you see.

The fact of the matter be
were are doing life in the
open.

Obstacles and death traps on
my back scoping.

Yeah. Yeah. Like crack
cocaine.

Leave your brain insane.

Like a dope fiends' vein.

It ain't hard to explain.

If the drugs don't catch you
the hustle side will.

Cause rude boys nowadays
stackin' ready to kill.

Domination of AIDS took over
third world countries and got
the f**king cheek to say

started by monkeys or was it created in a laboratory and necessary?

To divide third class with the upper class.

What the bumbarass?

Was I born this size cause your big conspiracy has to capsize.

Cause the people getting wise.

Can see through your disguise.

No more of your lies killing people like flies.

Have to realize your deadly combination trying to kill my black nation with your false information. Take this into consideration.

Incarceration of young black males believe crack sells, in the time of need.

Young baby needs to feed and you can't get a job.

You have to go out there and rob.

East Reflections

This poem East was just for anybody in East London. Around these times I was on road driving, I thought I was hottest thing around.

I wrote this as a message to any poet or rapper in East London who thought he had bars. It was just a let's do it rhyme ting. No matter where you come from, Hackney Leyton, Leytonstone, which was my end. Stratford, Plaistow, East Ham, Barking, Walthamstow, Chingford,

Custom House, Manor Park, Bow, White-chapel, Bethnal-Green, wherever in East London you was from, this one's for you.

East

Who was talking like the best in the East?

Get eat for a feast.

The belly of the beast.

Or the beast of the belly.

You wobble like jelly.

Knock back your Henny like you really need it.

Believe it this ain't no secret.

You can't leak it.

Peep it, f**king keep it.

No way you can teef it.

Nah, what's this, the war of words?

My words big and serious.

Leave your brain delirious.

Get box with the alphabet.

I'm a threat.

On your marks, get set, go.

Here's another flow.

A E I O U.

What you gonna do?

When I split your confidence.

With vows and consonants?

Won't tell you no nonsense.

Nah, something for nothing.

Nothing for something.

Push my button.

I'm glutton for these beats
and sounds.

Objective and nouns.

Words that are verbs.

Observe your nerves.

Mr. Man, you're a nerd but
not multi-milli.

You f**kers look silly really,
like Milli Vanilli when they

mime their songs. Run along Daddy Don.

Don't get this wrong.

Check a buff gyal in a thong, pumping my song.

I'm the bomb from 19 how long.

I was jacking, paper stacking.

6 deuce still clapping.

The 6 deuce release red juice.

If you try boost up your chest.

Leave you to rest.

Nothing less put it to the test.

Where is your vest?

Leave you stressed.

I guess manifest in the best.

Latest drop top.

Your pulse stop when my glock pop.

What?

Deuce.

Twisted Reflections

Twisted was a rhyme I put together just to show the mandem, I can do this too. I didn't really realize what I was saying with the words that I was spitting. I was just having fun putting words together, making them rhyme and seeing them make sense at the same time was intriguing. Then I started rhyming over beats and everything started to come together lyrically and I was impressed with myself.

Reciting my poetry to other people, making them feel my vibe. Twisted is an everyday rhyme for anyone whose brain got twisted along the way in life.

Twisted

Don't get it twisted.

Get your cap twisted.

Lifted like my fifth did.

Then I get spliffed.

Nah, never sold a ho.

I'm not a pimp.

Put in my pocket, get pass the shrimp.

Can't you see? I don't walk with a limp.

My attitude stinks.

I couldn't care less what you think.

Kick back yo, sip on your drink.

I wouldn't want you to blink.

Or at my trigger man I'm gonna wink.

Cause your stack's juvenile.
My stacks be old and grey.

I beg you don't play stack large like Giant Hay.

Which day put up your pay.

You want to stay wouldn't want you to stray.

Some suckers gone the wrong way.

Yo, think again, gon up the wrong avenue.

I'll eat you up and spit you out just like a savage do.

Far from a cannibal ball till I fall, living it tall like a skyscraper.

See ya later, push down accelerators.

Large engines your beat sounds very feminine.

There's no mending.

If it's broke sucker throw it away.

Hear what I say, shots spray.

By the a to the k pussy's laid today.

Or maybe tonight, whatever you like.

I'm telling you I ain't gonna fight.

Bruised up my fist for a whole lot a years.

Switch tables round leaving families in tears.

Got hug like bears leave you short of breath.

I know you rather die with your teff thought it was thicker.

Kick back and sip my liquor.

On a humble.

You want to chat to me don't mumble.

That man makes you stumble.

While he grumbles.

Shot him up, now you fumble to the floor.

That's what he's paid for.

Disrespect yo' and that's what you get laid for.

It's so f**k**g simple.

Four shots to your dimple.

Leave you wrinkle, crinkle, while I sprinkle weed into the rizla.

Meditate to Sizzler.

Rastafari, most high.

Negus please us.

Many say the Black Jesus.

We pull leavers of black sticks many tricks, you get fix if you wined up in the mix of my

nuzzle front let me put this
blunt don't ever take me for
no cunt to come pull that
stunt, but it's a new chapter.

You're an over reactor.

It's a plain factor.

I'm a fast reactor.

Slow reactor. I'll catch ya.

Ways Reflections

This poem I definitely didn't know what I was saying, but it somehow reflected the music industry so much. And then I realized the industry wasn't so easy, you have to be mentally and physically prepared for it. You just have to be ready for it no matter which angle it comes at you. If you want the money and the fame, prepare for the pain. That was a motto I used to use and ways was the poem I thought represented the bad boy in me. This is what I came up with.

Ways

Run come chase my ways.

My s**t be like a maze.

I can rhyme for days.

Jah know, spitting out phrases.

Leave your tongue locked in cages.

Nothing to say.

lyrical mac 10 or AK to spray my way.

Your s**t be like a play.

I know you've rehearsed it.

So run along reverse it.

And go back where you come from.

Round here you don't belong.

Was you looking for a career?

I don't think so, Don.

You better go back to busting your gun.

If you know how I'll give you the show how.

On the late-night prowl.

Make a fucker scream wow, when my gun go pow!

Dump you off in the canal
because your style was foul.

Then we get back to the most
stacks and hot tracks.

Hot gats they got two bodies.

Don't make it 3 (Three).

You don't want to get seen it's
obscene.

Check the team, there killers
are mean.

Mean for cream, on a daily
basis.

I'm not a racist.

I creep at night with a buff gyal in the bed or I'm aiming at your head.

Either way it's straight lead.

You and I

Reflections

This next poem I wrote was for my girl because she was the reason I even started writing rhymes. If it wasn't for her, I don't even think I would have found out I could do it. See my girl had this dream of becoming famous from she was 12-years-old and when we got together; she still had the same dream. Like me and my girl were best friends and our birthdays were both in

September. So we've seen a lot of good, happy, fun times together and we were together for a long time still. At the end of the day, the bottom line was she wanted to make something of her life, be somebody and that's what she did.

You and I

My darling dear.

How could it be that we found love eternally?

A love created out of nothing.

But there must've been something.

That kept us loving.

Let's find assumption.

Going back in the days.

My ignorance says.

Would leave you amazed.

Of this childish ways.

But you're just like me.

So you have days too.

One thing I knew.

We'll stick like glue.

Many nights of fuss and many nights of anger.

But far more nights of this love and tender.

I surrender not my soul, but my loving heart.

This art of emotion.

Creaming you with lotion.

As I take this motion.

To relax your mind.

Everything is just fine.

In this moment of time.

If I could turn back mine.

I would redress the whole thing.

Put on my bling and become your special King.

Love x

City of Sin

Reflections

Sin. This one is about bad things in life and how cash rules everything around me and that is the bottom line. If you ain't got money, you can't do s**t, you need it to live, basically. That's why the government gives it away every month to keep the world circulating, keep it moving. It there is no wonga nothing cannot work, they give money out to take it back in. It's like a giant hugs factory people have the choice of whatever to spend on. Then you get people who do other things to get money, to feed habits, to get in a higher position in life, to support their family and gain respect, you just don't know what the case could be. There are all sorts of things that you might have to go through to get to where you want to be in life and 9 times out of 10 sin always gets you there. They say Jesus died for our sin. Well, that's a whole lot of sin all around the world and even in religion there is sin, all religion I'm talking about. Science, psychic, numeral and philosophy, the four basic principles that tell you about life, so that's why I wrote this poem.

City of Sin

In the city of sin.

Sin become your best friend.

It's so hard to cope.

If you're broke and you only got dope.

It's worse if you smoke your own pope

Wicked turn wicked.

20 gee a hit bid.

Who's the victim?

I'll trick them, split them, ill omen, fit them.

Fibreglass spit them.

And move on to the next moron.

Who kept on acting strong.

When his money wasn't long.

So, welcome to the sin city.

Where a pretty young ho shooting chow for cash flow.

Human living is a liberty.

To really see how it really be.

No simple fees in getting pee's (money), prosperity, in sin mentality.

Being fatality reality.

For a salary.

Don't be mad at me.

Just true how it be.

I'm just glad to see people living casually.

You see the casualty.

My deepest sympathy.

Way Back Then...

Reflections

This poem was an agreement with myself to get these rhymes out somehow, some way. I did this through a book with the help of my bigger cousin Winnie and the grace of God. R.I.P my grandpa, Mr. Bayley.

Blessings to my two grandmas in the UK, my other grandpa in the Caribbean, my mum, my dad, my brothers, my little sister and my cousins. The whole of my bloodline, aunties, uncles, everyone who's my direct bloodline. Bless up every time.

Wayne Bayley, yuh done know.

Way Back Then...

From way back then I wrote these rhymes.

And only bout now I made it time.

To read all the signs I made up my mind.

I'm so divine.

Back up on my grind.

Yo, in connect with the music set.

Most respect.

Even if it's indirect.

I look a check for a thousand mil.

For real, I've got the will to thrill.

You know the deal so.

From way back then had the raw cut.

Had it in my brain all stored up.

Now I got a cup full of Hennessy.

High-grade herb for the medi gee you see.

And that's the realest talk, cause it was a long time ago since I put them together and in life be all you can and all you want to be. Take each day as it comes, one day at a time. Time is always ticking, it never stops, Big Ben!

To each and everyone, go good, I wish all of you the best, stay bless. One love every time. I hope you all enjoyed the rhymes, you get me and nuff love, bless.

Only Emanuel Selassie I.

Jah Rastafari!

About the Author

Wayne Bayley is a debut author who grew up on the tough streets of East London. He started writing poetry 2nd May 2004 and developed a passion for writing and reciting his work. Spoken word gave him an opportunity to express emotions that he felt at the time. His vision is for this book to be heard worldwide and to inspire other others particularly the man dem to use writing as a form or release. Having experienced a turbulent past, Wayne has settled down and works part time and is now optimistic for the future and building his new book business.

For performances bookings, and television appearances

e: bayleywayne198@gmail.com

Printed in Great Britain
by Amazon